Ripley's HUMAN BODY

Believe It or Not!®

RIPLEY PUBLISHING

a Jim Pattison Company

Written by Camilla de la Bedoyere
Consultant Dr Irfan Ghani

RIPLEY
PUBLISHING

Publisher Anne Marshall

Managing Editor Rebecca Miles
Picture Researcher James Proud
Editors Lisa Regan, Rosie Alexander
Assistant Editor Amy Harrison
Proofreader Judy Barratt
Indexer Hilary Bird

Art Director Sam South
Design Rocket Design (East Anglia) Ltd
Reprographics Stephan Davis

www.ripleys.com

ISBN 978-1-893951-46-4

10 9 8 7 6 5 4 3 2 1

Library of Congress Cataloging-in-Publication Data is
available.

Printed in China

Contents

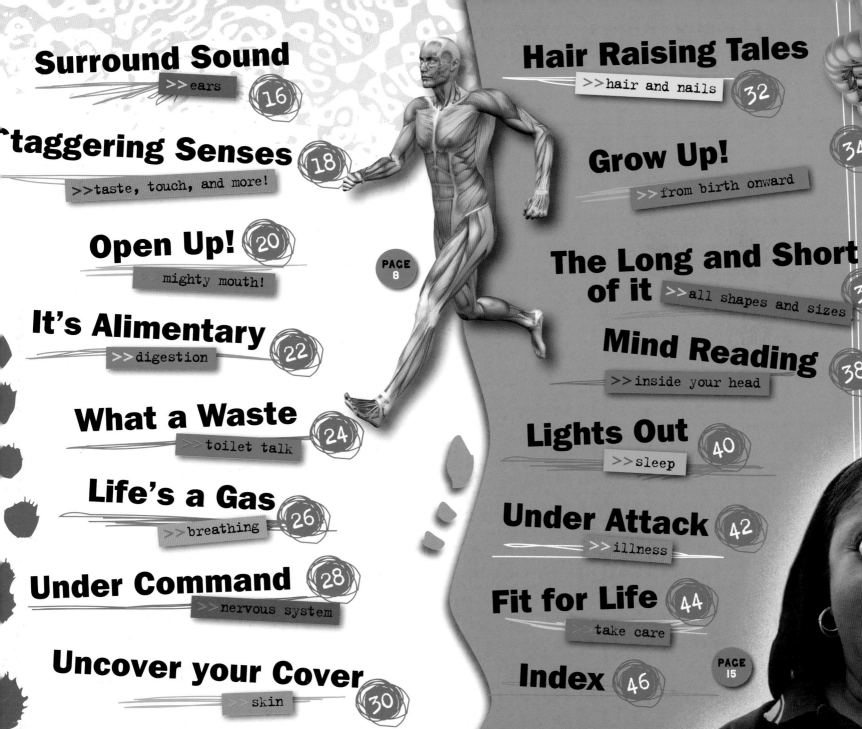

PAGE 8

PAGE 15

Body Beautiful

>> it's all about you >>

The human body is an amazing creation. A collection of bones, blood, and other vital bits, your body is just brilliant. There's so much going on inside your head and under your skin—things you know about, like doing your homework and eating your meals, and things you don't even have to think about, like breathing, bending, and going to the toilet.

This book will take you on a guided tour of the things that make you tick. Get to grips with how your muscles work, take a look inside an eyeball, and think about your brain and everything it does on a daily basis. Each page will open your eyes to the fantastic things going on in the human body, with special Ripley's fascinating facts and amazing 'Believe It or Not!' stories from around the world. What are you waiting for? Get stuck in!

Each year, nearly 7 million people in the US are treated for a broken bone.

The spine is made up of lots of odd-shaped bones called vertebrae (say ver-tuh-bray).

There is a hole in the middle of each vertebra, which the spinal cord fits through.

HERE TO HELP...
Of course, this book is packed full of fab facts and informative text—but look out for the five key features (numbered here). They will help you find out even more about your body—fun, facts, stories, it's all here!

The ribs form a protective cage (literally called the rib cage) around vital organs such as the heart and lungs. Most people have 12 pairs of ribs, making 24 altogether, but some people are born with only 11 pairs, and others get an extra rib or two!

TWISTS

Keep counting!

Father and son Albert and Karl Perculeza from the Philippines both boast extra digits. Each of them has 12 fingers and 12 toes!

Mind over matter

Shaolin monk warriors practice the art of meditation to help them overcome normal bodily sensations such as pain. This allows them to perform amazing feats such as lying on blades or nails.

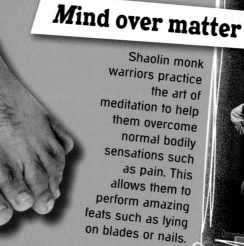

Ripley's Believe It or Not!

Check out these amazing stories! Take Marco Hort, for instance, from Switzerland, who managed to pack 264 drinking straws into his mouth. He had to dislocate his jaw to do it. Ouch!

2

BIG WORD ALERT! 3

...und a word that you don't understand? ...n't worry, there's a definition to help you. ...re's one to get you started: anatomy is ...e science that studies the way the human ...dy is put together.

Recipe time!

How to make a HUMAN BODY

Feeling like Frankenstein? Fancy making a new body?
You will need:

- **Bones** 206 bones for an adult or 350 for a baby
- **Blood** 1,000 teaspoons (0.9 gallons) of warm blood for a male body, but only 872 teaspoons (0.8 gallons) for a female
- **Oxygen** 1,500 ounces of oxygen – but most of that is in water, which is found in every cell of the body
- **Skin** 380 ounces of skin
- **Iron** 0.1 ounces of iron – that's enough to make a 3-inch nail
- **Carbon** 560 ounces of carbon – that's enough to make 900 pencils

Once your body is up and running, you will need to keep it in tip-top form. Follow this checklist to make sure it's all in working order. Does it:

Produce about ½ gallon of gas every day, as burps and farts?
Shed about 50,000 dead skin flakes every minute?
Make up to ½ gallon of urine, or pee, every day?
Breathe in air about 29,000 times a day?
Lose about 100,000 brain cells a day?
Make about 11 gallons of saliva (spit) every month?

twist it!

Your heart contains valves that open and close to allow blood to flow through. When they shut, they make the 'heartbeat' noise.

Your stomach is lined with mucus to protect it from its own strong digestive juices. It produces a new layer every two weeks to stop it from digesting itself.

To make room for your heart, your left lung is smaller than your right lung.

4

...book as it is and stand on your head, if that suits you better...

...fab facts about the subject. Or leave the ...reason—turn the page to read even more ...This book isn't in the TWISTS series for no ...Woah! The world has turned upside down!

TURNING HEADS

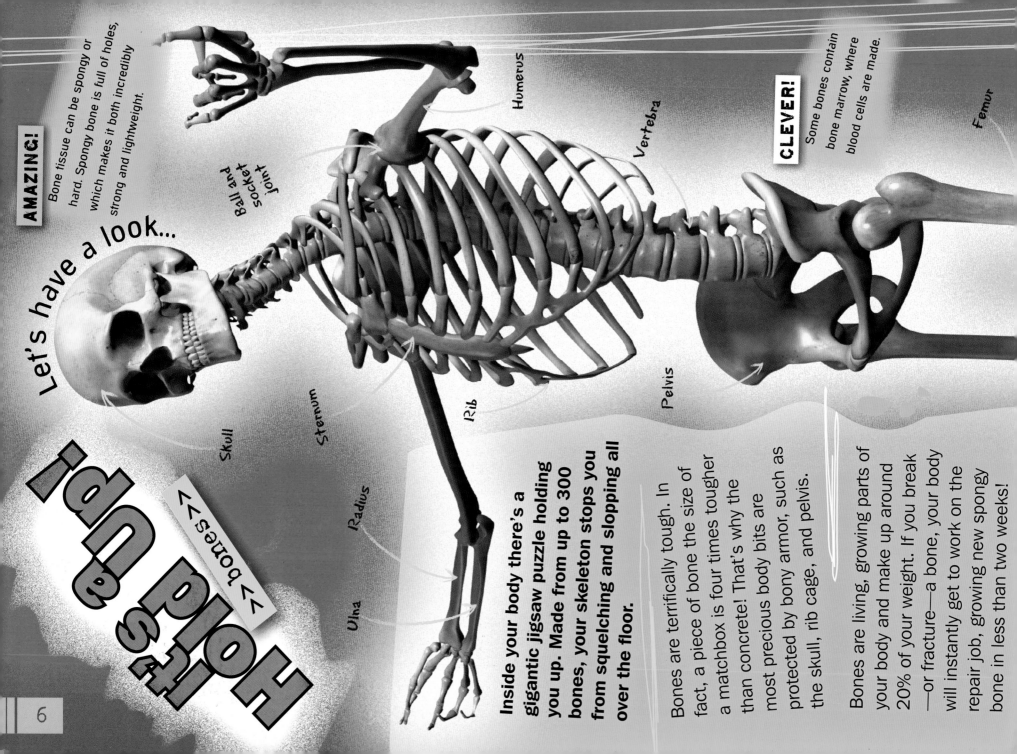

It's Hold UP!
>> bones >>

AMAZING!

Bone tissue can be spongy or hard. Spongy bone is full of holes, which makes it both incredibly strong and lightweight.

Let's have a look...

CLEVER!

Some bones contain bone marrow, where blood cells are made.

Labels:
Humerus
Vertebra
Ball and socket joint
Skull
Sternum
Rib
Radius
Ulna
Pelvis
Femur

Inside your body there's a gigantic jigsaw puzzle holding you up. Made from up to 300 bones, your skeleton stops you from squelching and slopping all over the floor.

Bones are terrifically tough. In fact, a piece of bone the size of a matchbox is four times tougher than concrete! That's why the most precious body bits are protected by bony armor, such as the skull, rib cage, and pelvis.

Bones are living, growing parts of your body and make up around 20% of your weight. If you break —or fracture—a bone, your body will instantly get to work on the repair job, growing new spongy bone in less than two weeks!

Ripley's Believe It or Not!

There are **206 bones** in an adult's body. Half of them are in the feet (52) and hands (54). Babies have around 300 soft bones, but some of these join together as the baby grows.

Minerals, such as calcium, make your bones hard. If you sucked all the minerals out of a leg bone, it wouldn't be much stronger than a piece of string.

Your bones are **softer than an adult's**. They won't fully harden until you are 18 years old.

You will probably bend—or flex—your finger joints more than **25 million times** in a lifetime: even more if you play a musical instrument!

Humans have tail bones. Called the coccyx (say cox-six), this part of your spine helps you lift heavy objects and keep balanced.

Most people have 12 pairs of ribs, making 24 in total. However, one person out of every 500 has 13 or 11 pairs instead!

Bones don't bend, but they do move where are places called tough meet. These joints connecting are held together ligaments are tissue called joints.

Hinge joint

Fibula

Tibia

Ray Gonzales

Twenty years ago amazingly flexible **Ray Gonzales** discovered that he had such flexilble joints that he could twist his body 180 degrees so that his feet point completely the wrong way. Great for walking backward!

DON'T TRY THIS AT HOME!

HOW LOW CAN YOU GO?

Limbo-skating, shown off here by Aniket Chindak from India, involves stretching your ligaments so much that the body can fold almost flat. With enough speed, Aniket can roller skate underneath a parked car!

Use the Force

No matter how much you grow, there are parts of your body that shrink—muscles! Thankfully, these bundles of mighty fibers only get smaller to move a bone, before returning to their normal size.

Muscles give you power; they make up half your body weight and provide the pulling forces that allow you to bend an arm or lift a foot. Without your muscles —whether they're feeble or fearsome—you simply wouldn't be able to move. You've got 100 just in your head, face, and neck!

PUCKER UP!

You use 11 face muscles to frown, 12 to smile, and 20 to kiss!

Muscles usually work in pairs. Bend your arm and flex your biceps to see the muscle bulge as it shortens. As you relax your arm the biceps relaxes and the triceps muscle below contracts (becomes shorter).

Bent arm—biceps is contracted.

MOVE IT!

There are three types of muscle. **Skeletal muscle** helps you move and **smooth muscle** does jobs such as keeping food traveling through your digestive system. **Cardiac muscle** makes your heart pump blood. Skeletal muscles are attached to bones by tough fibers, called tendons.

The triceps muscle will contract to straighten the arm again.

MEGA MUSCLES

Turn your foot outward and you will be using 13 different muscles in your leg and 20 in the foot. Taking a simple step forward uses 54 muscles!

Humans have more than 600 muscles in their bodies, but caterpillars have more than 4,000!

Your body is about two-thirds water, and about half of this is contained in your muscles.

The tiniest muscle in the body is called the stirrup. You have one inside each ear, and it is no bigger than this number 1.

Way back in the 1920s performer Clarence Willard amazed audiences by growing 6 inches in height, just by stretching the muscles of his knees, hips, and throat.

← twist it!

Xie Tianzhuang, an 87 year old from China, lifted 14 bricks with his teeth in 2005. The bricks weighed a total of 77 pounds.

Need a lift? Ask John Evans! He could possibly carry you and your car on his head! His best effort is balancing a car weighing 353 pounds for 33 seconds.

need a lift?

Keep on truckin'

The Rev. Jon Bruney, from Indiana, USA, is famous for his strongman achievements, such as bending steel bars and tearing phone directories in half. In 2004 he and two other strongmen joined forces to pull a 16-ton trailer for 10.9 miles.

BIG WORD ALERT!

GLUTEUS MAXIMUS
The biggest muscle in your body is called the gluteus maximus. It's in your buttocks.

Under Pressure

>>blood>>

Blood: you know it as the oozy red liquid that pours out when you cut yourself. But about 1.3 gallons of this thick juice is racing around your body, keeping everything in good order. Lose half of your blood and you'll drop dead!

Blood is like a river of life. It carries oxygen and nutrients to every cell, and mops up all the toxic waste. It's also at the front line of your body's defense system. White blood cells track down and kill any nasty bugs that are out to damage, or even destroy, you.

There are five types of white blood cell. They patrol your body on the lookout for bacteria, viruses, cancer cells, and other unwanted visitors.

Blood is made up of red cells, white cells, and parts of cells called platelets.

Blood cells float in a fluid called plasma. Blood makes up about 8% of your body weight.

CRUSTY!

Scabs are made up of dried, clotted, blood and dead skin cells that stick together making a natural Band-Aid™.

Red blood cells use iron to transport oxygen. That's why you need this mineral (found in meat and some vegetables) in your diet.

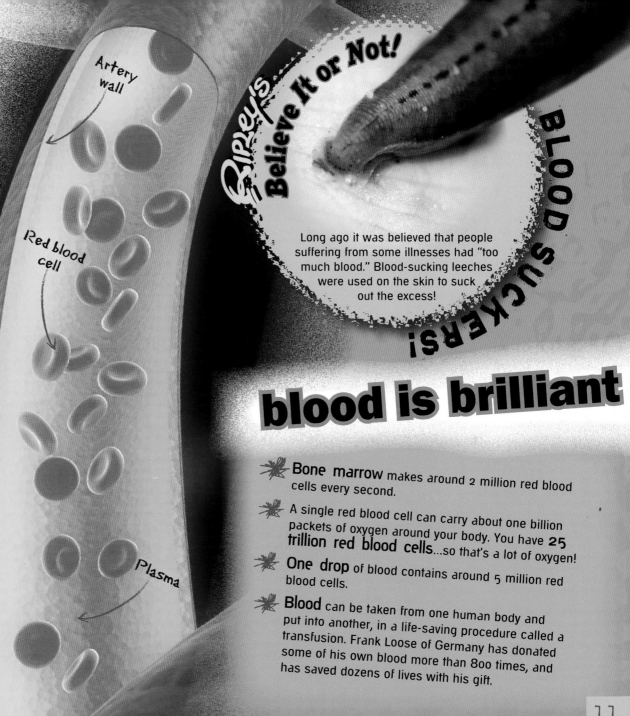

NUTRIENTS

Substances that provide goodness for growth and health, like fats, proteins, and carbohydrates. One of the roles of blood is to carry nutrients around the body.

Surgeons operating on a man in Vancouver, Canada, in 2007, were used to the sight of blood, but not dark green in color! Doctors think it turned that color because of medication the patient was taking.

Artery wall

Red blood cell

Plasma

Ripley's Believe It or Not!

Long ago it was believed that people suffering from some illnesses had "too much blood." Blood-sucking leeches were used on the skin to suck out the excess!

BLOOD SUCKERS!

blood is brilliant

- **Bone marrow** makes around 2 million red blood cells every second.

- A single red blood cell can carry about one billion packets of oxygen around your body. You have **25 trillion red blood cells**...so that's a lot of oxygen!

- **One drop** of blood contains around 5 million red blood cells.

- **Blood** can be taken from one human body and put into another, in a life-saving procedure called a transfusion. Frank Loose of Germany has donated some of his own blood more than 800 times, and has saved dozens of lives with his gift.

Take Heart

In the center of your chest is your heart. It's a powerful, pumping organ that sends blood rushing around a network of blood vessels at speeds of 167 miles a day!

When your heart beats it pumps blood from inside the heart around your body, through blood vessels. In between beats your heart fills with blood again. Your blood carries oxygen to all parts of your body to make them work. It gets this oxygen from your lungs when you breathe in. This oxygen-rich blood is taken to your heart to be pumped around the body.

When the blood has delivered the oxygen to your body it comes back to the heart to be pumped out again to collect more oxygen from the lungs.

BODY PUMP

aorta
carries oxygen-rich blood to the body

pulmonary artery
takes blood to the lungs, to collect oxygen

right atrium
blood from the body enters the heart here

left atrium
receives oxygen-rich blood from the lungs

left ventricl
pumps bloc to the bo through t aorta

Your heart beats around 60–80 times a minute, but doing exercise can increase this rate to 200 times a minute!

right ventricle
pumps the blood to the lungs

12

blood vessels

There are two types of large blood vessel. Arteries (shown in red) carry blood away from the heart. Veins (shown in blue) carry blood toward the heart. There are both veins and arteries in all parts of the body.

A boy called Goga Diasamidze from Tbilisi in Georgia was born with two hearts. The second of them is near his stomach and works perfectly well.

FASCINATING FACT!

HEART OF THE MATTER

Blood vessels connect your heart with all your body parts. If you could lay these tubes in one long line, they would measure 62,100 miles and would circle the world more than twice!

At any moment, about 75% of your blood is in your veins, but only 5% is in your capillaries. The remaining 20% is in your arteries.

Capillaries are tiny blood vessels. They connect arteries to veins, and make up 98% of the total length of all blood vessels.

Your heart will beat more than 3 billion times if you live to old age and will have pumped enough blood to fill an oil tanker 46 times over!

BRRR!

Many of 'Ice Man' Wim Hof's amazing feats take place in icy conditions. Here, he stood in 1,550 pounds of ice for an incredible 1 hour 12 minutes! He has mastered the ability to increase his heart rate and the blood flow to his extremities (like his fingers and toes) to stop the cold affecting him as badly.

CORONARY
To do with the heart.

CIRCULATORY
The network of blood vessels and heart—and the way they send blood around and around the body—is called a circulatory system.

BIG WORD ALERT!

Seeing is Believing
>> eyes >>

Eyes are jelly-filled cameras and your body's number-one sense organs. All day long your eyes keep your brain busy, passing it masses of information about the world around you.

Rays of light pour into your eyes, where clear lenses focus them to make a crisp, clean image. Nerves pass info about the image to the brain, which has the tricky task of turning those nerve signals into vision. It can even combine the images from both eyes to make a single 3-D picture.

It takes six muscles to move each eyeball, so you can get a good view all around. If you spy something sad, your tears drain into tiny holes in the corner of your eyes, and flow into your nose. That's why your nose runs when you cry!

14

HUMORS
The _aqueous_ and _vitreous humors_ are clear substances (either watery or like jelly) in the eyeball.

BIG WORD ALERT!

TAKE A LOOK

- Vitreous humor
- Reti[na]
- Lens
- Aqueous humor
- Ligaments
- Pupil
- Iris
- Cornea

EYE SPY
Human eye muscles move around 10,000 times a day!

Eyes are delicate organs, so we have eyelids, eyelashes, and tears to protect them.

twist it!

The muscles you use to blink are the fastest in your body, moving your eyelids at a speedy 14 inches a second around 84 million times every year!

You lose around 1,600 of your eyelashes each year. Thankfully, new ones are always growing.

It's impossible to sneeze with your eyes open.

A newborn baby can't make tears until it is around three weeks old!

The retina has about 130 million cells for seeing black and white, but only 7 million for seeing colors. Humans can detect 500 shades of gray!

WOOOOAHHH!

A visual (or optical) illusion tricks us into seeing something that isn't real. Look at this picture, let your eyes roam from circle to circle, and it will appear to have moving parts. Of course, it doesn't, but sometimes your brain can't quite keep up with messages sent by your eyes.

The colored part of your eye is called the iris. It controls how much light enters the pupil, to produce perfect images, and protects your eyes from sun damage.

tic
rve

Student Jalisa Mae Thompson can pop her eyeballs so far

out of their sockets they hardly look real!

15

Surround Sound

>> ears >>

Listen carefully—it's time to find out how ears hear. These auditory organs don't just help you to sense sound: they stop you from falling over, every time you take a step!

That fleshy flap stuck to the side of your head is just one part of an ear. Each flap, or pinna, sends sound down your ear canal to the eardrum, which vibrates. Those vibrations shimmy through the tiny hammer, anvil, and stirrup bones into a shell-shaped organ, called the cochlea.

The cochlea is where the real business of hearing happens. Sound is turned into nerve impulses and sent at lightning speed to the brain. And hey presto: you can hear!

Your smallest bones—stirrups—are in your ears. They measure 0.1 inch long and weigh 0.0001 oz.

Hammer

Semicircular canals

Anvil

Auditory nerve

To the brain

Here-hear!

Pinna

Ear canal

Eardrum

Stirrup

Cochlea

OUCH!

Playing a personal music player (MP3) on full volume could permanently damage your hearing after just 1 minute 29 seconds.

The cochlea contains millions of tiny hairs. When vibrations make them move, they send messages to the brain along the auditory nerve.

GET THE BALANCE RIGHT

Squashed next to the cochlea is an organ of balance. It is made up of three tubes, all filled with liquid. If you spin around, that liquid swirls about, making you dizzy!

STEADY AS YOU GO

Balancing on a high wire is tricky enough, but this guy managed to pedal his bike 100 feet above the ground without falling off!

SOUNDS AMAZING

Beethoven was a famous composer of classical music. He continued to write and perform great music even when he lost his hearing!

Wei Mingtang from China has leaky ears. He attaches a hose to them, and then blows out candles or inflates balloons!

Earwax and ear hair protect your ears, and even prevent insects from nesting in the ear canal!

Earwax can be yellow, orange, or brown and gross old bits drop out of your ears all the time.

People used to believe that earwigs would climb into ears while people slept, and burrow into their brains to lay their eggs. It's not true, honestly!

twist it!

It may sound strange (ha ha!) but many people around the world enjoy performing feats of "ear strength." This man, celebrating Chinese New Year in Beijing, is just one of several who chooses to pull vehicles along with his ear. Ouch!

Hey, you've got something in your ear! Narayan Rasad Pal of India proudly shows off the long strands of hair that grow from his ears. They measure an incredible 4 inches!

BIG WORD ALERT!

AUDITORY

To do with hearing.

Staggering Senses

>> taste, touch, and more! >>

Close your eyes and touch the tip of your nose with a finger. Easy, isn't it? But how did you know where your nose is? Thanks to your staggering senses you've got up-to-date nuggets of info passing to your brain all of the time.

How many senses do you have? People used to say we have five: we can see, hear, touch, smell, and taste. But now we know there are plenty more. Feelings such as cold and hunger are all part of your body's sensory world.

RUMBLE!

Got tummy rumbles and pain in your belly? Your body is telling you to eat—now! You could make like Japan's Takeru Kobayashi, international champion hot-dog eater. In 2005 he retained his title by eating 49 hot dogs in 12 minutes. His personal best is an unbelievable 53.5 hot dogs in that time!

BRRR!

Getting so cold it hurts? Time to put on your winter clothes or go somewhere warm, before you freeze to death. Ice swimmer Lewis Pugh swam 0.6 miles in the Antarctic wearing only a swimming cap, goggles, and trunks, in a temperature of 32°F. He was in the water for 18 minutes 10 seconds and described the feeling as a "screaming pain all over his body."

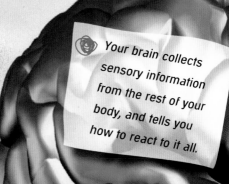

Your brain collects sensory information from the rest of your body, and tells you how to react to it all.

YUM!

Taste is an important sense—it can warn you that something isn't good for you to put in your mouth.

FASCINATING FACT

An ice-cream parlor in Nice, France, offers its customers up to 70 different flavors of ice cream, including tomato and basil, black olive, and chewing gum!

OUCH!

Some pains keep you from harm or tell you it's time to visit the doctor. Not so for Miss Electra, who had 2 million volts of electricity passed through her body and out of her fingertips for a TV show in Hollywood. She doesn't feel any pain when this takes place!

Your senses are there to tell your brain what is going on inside, and outside, the body.

Your brain then knows if things are changing, and can decide when to make your body react—perhaps to keep you safe, or get some food or drink, for example.

The information is sent to your brain along nerves.

SNIFF!

Pongs and stenches tell us to stay away—stinky food might be covered in nasty bacteria. Mind you, blue cheese such as Stilton smells strong but is safe to eat. The blue veins are mold caused by bacteria, and if you think they smell like smelly feet, you'd be right: it can be the same bacteria.

FASCINATING FACT

The makers of Stilton cheese have launched their own perfume with the same smell!

OOPS!

Stumbling, tripping, and falling over—it happens to us all, but most of the time your body is great at keeping your limbs in the right place, and balanced. Shame it only goes wrong when everyone is looking!

FASCINATING FACT

It takes just 0.02 of a second for your brain to realize when you have dropped a book on your toe.

Open Up!

>>mighty mouth!>>

Your mouth is home to 10,000 taste buds, up to 32 teeth, and billions of bacteria. In fact, there are more bacteria in your mouth than there are people on the planet!

A mouth is a dark hole with lots of jobs to do, from chewing and crunching to coughing, swallowing, tasting, and talking. Food begins its digestive journey in your mouth, where teeth grind it into little pieces and morsels get juiced up with sloppy saliva. Thanks to the taste buds on your tongue you can sense flavors—such as salty, sour, sweet, and bitter—and either enjoy your snack-attack, or choose to spit out yucky bits.

INSIDE A TOOTH

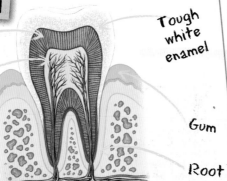

Dentine

Pulp (contains nerves and blood vessels)

Tough white enamel

Gum

Root

SALIVA
Spit! The gooey substance made by your mouth. In fact, your mouth produces about ¼ gallon of the stuff every day. Eeoogh!

BIG WORD ALERT!

Incisor

Gum

Lips

Uvula

Tonsil

Tongue

Molar

Premolar

Canine

BABY TEETH
Your teeth started growing about six months before you were born!

20

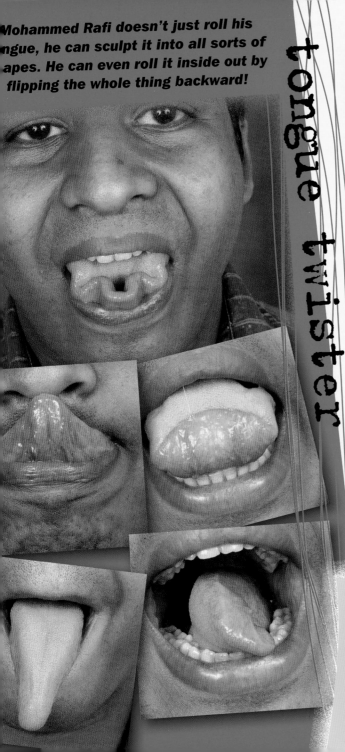

Mohammed Rafi doesn't just roll his tongue, he can sculpt it into all sorts of shapes. He can even roll it inside out by flipping the whole thing backward!

KEY FACTS

→ There are more than **500 types of bacteria** in your mouth. Most of them are helpful bugs, but the bad ones can rot your teeth or give you bad breath.

→ You use your jaws, lips, and tongue to speak. Babies' first sounds include **"coo," "ba ba,"** and **"da da."**

→ **Girls are usually better** at identifying flavors than boys, but boys prefer stronger flavors than girls. Teenagers don't like sour-tasting food!

Ripley's Believe It or Not!

TOOTH ART

These tiny tattoos of famous people have been done on teeth!

LONG LICK

Annika Irmler from Germany has a tongue that measures 2¾ inches. It is so long she can lick ice cream from the bottom of an ice-cream cone.

TOOTHY GRIN

Babies are usually born with no teeth, although it isn't rare for a newborn to have one or two. Sean Keeney from England was born in 1990 with 12 of his teeth already!

TASTY!

Stephen Taylor from the UK has a 3¾-inch tongue: long enough to touch his own nose AND to lick his own nostrils!

21

It's Alimentary

>>digestion>>

Your digestive system is a fabulous food processor. It pulps and pulverizes food before squirting it with burning acids and churning it into a stinking stomach soup that is forced through your gurgling guts (also known as intestines).

Billions of bacteria break the food down into smaller and smaller bits so they can be used to fuel your body and help it grow.

A sandwich's journey through your alimentary canal—from mouth to anus—can take more than 24 hours and covers around 23 feet in total.

It's big!

The small intestine is lined with tiny, finger-like villi. On the surface of the villi are even tinier folds called microvilli. If you stretched all your villi out they would cover a football field!

Esophagus

Stomach

Pancreas

Gall bladder

Appendix

Anus

Small intestine (ileum)

Large intestine (colon)

KEY FACTS

※ Your **alimentary canal** is packed with chemicals called enzymes. These powerful juices help break food down into useful nutrients.

※ The **esophagus** is a tube that leads from your mouth to your stomach. It's made of muscles that force the food downward.

※ Your **gall bladder** and **pancreas** store and produce substances that help the body's digestive process.

※ After a big meal your stomach can stretch to **40 times** the size it was when it was empty.

※ One type of bacteria called **Heliobacter pylori** survives in the stomach's burning juices. These mini-bugs infect half of the world's people, and can cause pain and ulcers.

Sonya Thomas is America's competitive eating champion. She weighs just 99 pounds, but has managed to gulp down 46 mince pies in ten minutes and 52 hard-boiled eggs in just five!

LIVE SCORPIONS

Father-of-two Hasip Kaya of Turkey has been addicted to eating live scorpions since he was a boy.

FLY FEAST

In protest at his town's garbage collection service, a man named Farook, from Tirunelveli, India, started eating nothing but flies.

LIVE TREE FROGS AND RATS

For over 40 years, Jiang Musheng of China has eaten live tree frogs and rats to ward off abdominal pains.

CHICKEN FEED

Jan Csovary, from Prievidza, Slovakia, eats chicken for breakfast, lunch, and dinner, and has consumed over 12,000 chickens since the early 1970s.

NOTHING BUT CHEESE

Dave Nunley from Cambridgeshire, England, has eaten nothing but grated mild cheddar cheese for more than 25 years and gets through 238 pounds of it every year.

DIET OF WORMS

Wayne Fauser from Sydney, Australia, eats live earthworms.

CRAZY

If you unraveled your esophagus, stomach, and intestines they would reach the height of a three-story building.

The acids in your stomach are so strong they could dissolve a razor blade!

During the course of your life you will produce enough saliva (that's your spit) to fill a swimming pool.

Whenever you blush, the lining of your stomach gets redder too.

Half a million new stomach cells are made every minute!

It takes more brainpower to work your thumb than to control your stomach.

twist it!

Michel Lotito

eats bicycles, televisions, and even aircraft with no problems! He has to take them apart and slurp down mineral oil before swallowing the smaller bits.

DON'T TRY THIS AT HOME!

23

What a Waste

As your food makes its way through your digestive system, your body makes sure that nothing it needs goes to waste. A team of friendly organs slogs away, like a recycling plant, to suck out every last bit of goodness.

Blood vessels carry the nutrients from your food to the liver, where they are sorted, processed, recycled, or stored. The useless bits are sent packing back to your guts where they join the leftovers to make the solid stuff that leaves your body. It's called feces (say fee-sees).

Feces is made up of old blood cells, pieces of undigested food, bacteria, and water. The liquid waste is called urine and it's actually 96% water.

24

aorta
A giant blood vessel that carries oxygen-rich blood to the organs of the body.

inferior vena cava
A blood vessel that takes oxygen-poor blood back to the heart.

two kidneys
These work like filters to sort out toxic waste and remove it. They also send unwanted water to the bladder.

liver
The largest organ inside the body and, with your guts, helps to sort out the good stuff from the waste.

ureters
Long tubes that push liquid waste from the kidneys to the bladder.

bladder
A stretchy sack that holds urine until you are ready to pee it out.

urethra
A tube that takes urine from the bladder to outside the body.

- The liver has more than 500 different jobs, including cleaning blood, storing vitamins, and preparing nutrients to be used by the body.

- If you don't drink enough water your kidneys stop water going into your bladder. That makes your wee look darker.

- Minerals in urine can turn into solid stones, called bladder stones, which have to be removed by a doctor.

WASTE PRODUCTS

Even waste is recycled. Feces and urine travel from toilets through sewage pipes to sewage plants, where waste matter can be turned into fabulous fertilizer to be spread on farmers' fields.

Many ancient people believed that drinking their own urine would cure tummy troubles or other digestive disorders. Romans used it in their toothpaste.

One person produces enough urine to fill about 270 bathtubs during a lifetime.

Your liver is the second largest organ of your body and it can continue to work if 80% of it is removed. It will even grow back to its previous size!

twist it!

There are more than one million tiny tubes, or filters, in the kidneys. They are called nephrons and measure around 40 miles in total length!

FUNNY TUMMY

Sloppy poo is called diarrhea (say die-ar-ee-ah). It's often caused by nasty bugs – so wash your hands before eating and after using the loo!

TIME FOR TEA

A restaurant in Kaohsiung, China, is totally toilet themed. Diners sit on toilets, eat at basin-style tables, and have their food served in bowls shaped like toilets or waste pots.

FEELING FLUSHED!

Imagine finding a snake in your toilet! A 10-foot-long boa constrictor showed up in a toilet bowl in Manchester, England, and reappeared in a neighbor's bathroom after moving through the apartment complex's sewage system.

CLEAN MACHINE!

This wacky flying machine was part of a 2003 flying demonstration in France. Don't flush while you're up there!

TOILET TALK

25

Life's a Gas

>> breathing >>

Oxygen: you can't see it, smell it, touch it, or taste it, but without this gas your body would pack up in minutes. Thanks to your lungs you can concentrate on other things while you breathe in oxygen—more than 10 million times every year!

Lungs are lazy life-savers. With no muscles of their own, these air-filled puffers rely on rib muscles and a diaphragm to work. Every breath you take draws air into your lungs, which are each packed with 300 million alveoli. These thin-skinned sacs are swap shops, where oxygen is traded for carbon dioxide, the waste gas you breathe out.

BIG WORD ALERT!

RESPIRATION

Breathing in and out. All the body parts that get oxygen from the air, and pass it into the blood stream, are called the respiratory system.

Air-mazing

Air contains 21% oxygen. Breathing pure oxygen is actually dangerous.

look inside your lungs!

BREATHE OUT

BREATHE IN

Trachea

Bronc

Bronchus

Bronchioles

At the top of the trachea is a voice box, or larynx. Passing air through the larynx as you breathe out makes your vocal cords vibrate, creating sound. Breathing in and talking at the same time is almost impossible—try it!

Left lung

Right lung

Phew!

With six billion people breathing in oxygen you may expect we'd run out one day. Fortunately, when green plants respire they use up carbon dioxide, and produce oxygen. Phew!

DEEP BREATH

You breathe around 20 times a minute: that's 700 million times during an average lifetime.

Every day you breathe in enough air to fill 1,000 party balloons. (But we don't recommend it!)

Your lungs contain around 300,000 capillaries (tiny blood vessels). If they were stretched out they would measure 1,490 miles!

The loudest scream ever measured was 129 decibels: that's loud enough to make your ears hurt.

twist it!

LUNGS—
LET'S LOOK CLOSER

Bronchiole

Artery from heart

Deoxygenated blood from heart

Oxygenated blood to heart

Alveoli

David Merlini spent 10 minutes 17 seconds chained and handcuffed underwater in 2007, without air. He escaped from the five sets of handcuffs and 60 pounds of chains all without taking a single breath.

In June, 2008, freediver Herbert Nitsch from Austria used just the air in his lungs to sink to a record-breaking 702 feet in the ocean. During the dive, which took 4 minutes 24 seconds, his lungs shrank to the size of a fist and filled with blood, returning to normal at the surface.

Under Command

Electrical messages buzz around your body at speeds of 328 feet per second—that's ten times faster than the fastest human has ever run, and about one-third of the speed of sound.

These speedy signals zap backward and forward on the body's super-highways— your nerves—and are controlled by the brain. You've got a lot of nerve: if all of your body's nerves were spread end to end they would measure more than 93,200 miles!

Nerves instruct muscles to move, and send back messages to the brain about what's happening to your body. Like a strict principal, they have everything under their command.

A thick nerve cable—the spinal cord—runs up through the center of your spine to your brain. It's kept safe and snug inside a column of backbones.

nervous twitch?

Your brain and all your nerves together make up the nervous system. This is your body's main command and control center.

Muscle fiber

Nerve cell

Axon

Nerves are like long cables o electrical wire They are made up of nerve cells, called neurons.

Junction between nerve cell and muscle

TWIST IT!

ON YOUR NERVES

Toddlers and teenagers have far more neurons (nerve cells) than adults or kids of other ages.

NOT FUNNY

The nerves in your elbow run close to the skin, which is why a knock to your "crazy bone" feels so weird.

Professor Kevin Warwick studies robot technology. He has had silicon chips inserted into his body, which connect his nervous system to a computer. Now he can control doors and lights without lifting a finger!

The longest cells in your body are found in your brain. Stretched out, each one would measure up to 33 feet long.

If you burn your hand, your nerves swing into action, instructing your muscles to move it to safety in just 0.01 seconds.

LOOK OUT!

Catch! Entertainer Nathan Zorchak lives on his nerves, juggling with three chain saws whirring past his nose!

STEADY!

You want quick reactions? Look no further than Australian Anthony Kelly, who can catch flying arrows and, wearing a blindfold, stop speeding paintballs!

SNAKE KISSER

In Malaysia in 2006, Shahimi Abdul Hamid kissed a wild, venomous king cobra 51 times in three minutes, using his quick reflexes to dodge bites from the 16-foot snake.

Uncover your Cover

>> skin >>

No thicker than 20 pages of this book, yet making up 16% of your weight, your skin works hard for your body!

Here are just some of its jobs: it stops your body soaking up water like a sponge, prevents your blood from boiling or freezing, keeps bugs and bacteria out of your insides, and even senses pain and touch. But that's not all: 50 million bacteria call your skin home!

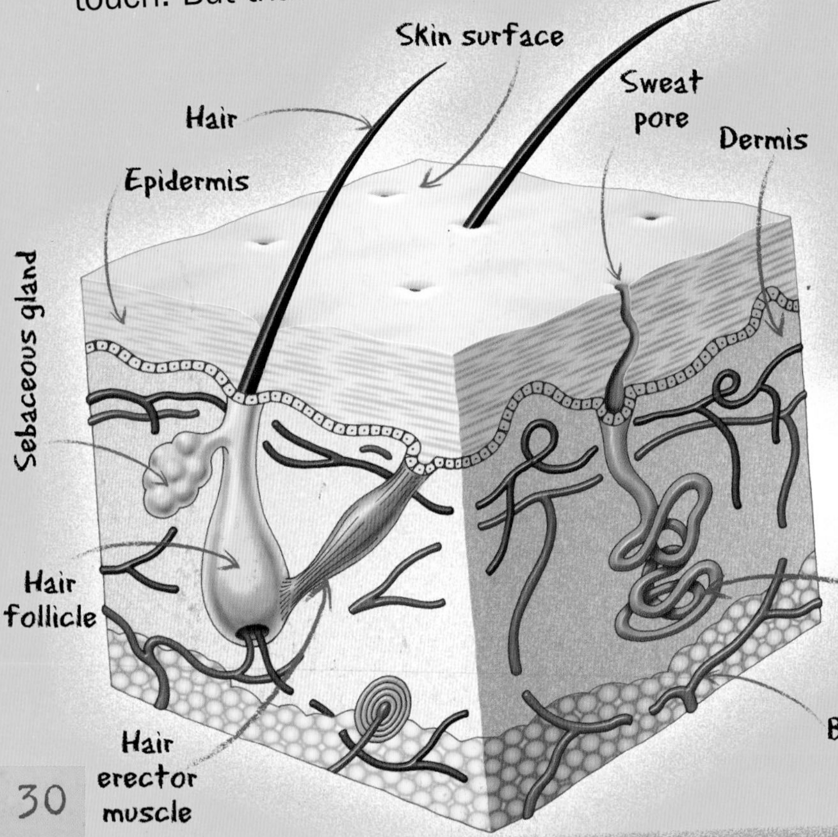

Skin is the body's largest organ and a piece no larger than a postage stamp holds 650 sweat glands, 20 blood vessels, and 1,000 nerve endings.

Sweat glands in your skin help to control temperature. When you are hot they ooze sweat, which is 99% water and 1% salt. As sweat evaporates, or dries, it cools your skin.

GROSS!

A million dust mites live in your mattress and pillow. They feed on the dead skin cells that fall off your body at night.

DON'T BE BLUE

Except Paul Karason can't help it. His skin has turned blue after treating a skin complaint with an ointment containing silver. He has also been drinking "colloidal silver" for about 15 years, which may have helped with his color change. It might even have turned his insides blue, too!

Skin diagram labels:
- Skin surface
- Hair
- Epidermis
- Sebaceous gland
- Hair follicle
- Hair erector muscle
- Sweat pore
- Dermis
- Sweat gland
- Blood vessels

BIG WORD ALERT!

EPIDERMIS
The top layer of your skin is called the epidermis. It is made from dead cells that are shed every 27 days.

SKIN FACTS

Feet sweat because there are 250,000 pores (tiny holes) in the soles. Each squirts about 12 teaspoons of sweat a day.

If you could peel off an adult's skin and stretch it out on the floor it would measure around 16 to 22 square feet, and weigh as much as 8.8 pounds.

A computer mouse has been invented that can sense people's emotions. By measuring changes in the user's skin, such as sweat and temperature, the mouse can tell if he or she is feeling sad, angry, or tired.

Lady Gray Rosemary Jacobs of the USA has gray skin. She thinks the change of color happened after she used nose drops, which contained tiny amounts of the metal silver.

twist it!

Meet the Leopard Man of Skye! The skin of Tom Leppard from Scotland has been tattooed with the markings of the big cat; over 99% of his skin is tattooed, with only the insides of his ears and the bits between his toes having no artwork.

Stretch it!

Gary Stretch has a rare skin condition that allows him to stretch it...and stretch it...and stretch it some more. His skin cells are affected so they don't hold together as tightly as they should, and his skin appears very loose on parts of his body.

Hair Raising Tales

>>hair and nails>>

Hair today, gone tomorrow! Most of your body is covered in strands of hair, which grow at a snail's pace of just a third of an inch a month. After a few years, each strand of hair falls out.

Thankfully, new hairs grow from special cells in your skin, called follicles, all the time. Each follicle can make about 20 new hairs in a lifetime. Hair grows fastest in the summer, but those dozy follicles like to slow down during the night and catch some zzzz. Both hair and nails are made from dead cells that are toughened with a protein called keratin, which is surprisingly stretchy.

Testing 1-2-3
Scientists can use one strand of hair to find out a person's age, sex, and race.

BIG HAIR!
Aaron Studham sports a magnificent Mohawk hairstyle that reaches 20 inches in height. It takes him an hour (and lots of hairspray) to get the look.

ITCHY
Tran van Hay from Vietnam has not cut his hair for 38 years and it now measures a staggering 20.3 feet. He wears it coiled around his head, which keeps the hair tidy, and his head warm.

snip-its and cuttings

HAIR FACE

Larry Gomez was born with a very rare medical condition, which causes thick, dark hair to grow all over his face and body.

- Human hair was used to make soy sauce in some Chinese barber shops, until the government banned it!

- Your toenails contain traces of gold!

- Mats made from human hair were used in San Francisco to mop up oil that had leaked into the San Francisco Bay.

- Blond people have about 130,000 hairs on their heads. People with red, black, or brown hair have up to 40,000 fewer.

SCRATCHY!

Lee Redmond has been growing her fingernails since 1979. She said it was tough trying to open doors or get dressed, but was very proud when her talons reached 33 inches! Sadly, Lee was involved in a car crash in 2009 and her nails all broke off.

Speedy
Fingernails grow about four times faster than toenails.

KEY FACTS

You could live without hair or nails, but they are useful. Hair helps to keep you warm, and nails protect your delicate fingertips from damage—and are handy when you have an itch!

You have hair all over your body except on the palms of your hands, the soles of your feet, and your lips. Humans have as many hairs as chimpanzees!

Blond, brunette, raven-haired, or redhead? You get your hair color thanks to the skin pigment, melanin.

33

Grow Up!

>> from birth onward >>

In about 270 days, or 38 weeks, a single cell can grow into a perfect human baby!

At birth the baby weighs around 7½ pounds and measures a mere 20 inches from head to toe—but will increase in weight a massive ten times by the age of ten. From ten to 20 this blooming baby will double in weight and should reach around 5½ feet tall.

Ageing is a one-way road, which eventually leads to death. Most people can expect to live into their seventies, although there are some supercentenarians (aged over 110 years) alive today.

Heave!

Two-year-old Salvador Quini, from Argentina, could lift weights heavier than himself—not so much a strongman as a strongboy!

ALL CHANGE

The time of growth, when kids develop into adults, is called puberty.

TINY TOT

Babies are supposed to develop inside their mother's womb for 37 to 40 weeks, but tiny Amillia Sonja Taylor was born after only 21 weeks and 6 days. She was just 9½ inches long.

MARVELOUS MIRACLE!

day 1 — Size of a pin's head

6 weeks — Size of a lentil

10 weeks — Size of a strawberry

16 weeks — Size of a pear

34

Three babies are born into the world every second.

Babies born on the island of Bali are not normally named until they are three months old. Before then, they are all called "mouse!"

Souleymane Mamam of Togo was just 13 years old when he played a soccer World Cup qualifier match against Zambia.

Thanks to the body's amazing ability to heal and grow, surgeons are able to stitch new body parts on to people, including arms and faces. Hearts, lungs, and kidneys can also be transplanted.

"Red" Rountree was 80 years old when he first decided to rob a bank in the USA. He carried on with his life of crime until he was 92, when he was finally locked up in prison!

twist it!

WORLD'S OLDEST

George Blair, or "Banana George" to his friends, is the world's oldest barefoot waterskiier. Age hasn't stopped him trying new challenges: he learned to snowboard when he was 75, drove his first racing car aged 81, and made his first parachute jump at 82!

SUPER BABY!

Mexican newborn Antonio Cruz weighed a massive 14 pounds when he was born—about twice the weight of many new babies. Look how big he is compared to the average-size baby lying next to him!

38 weeks

The baby is developed and ready to be born in the next few days or weeks.

30 weeks

The baby can open and close its eyes, and has eyelashes.

weeks

The baby can now hear its mother talking.

Circle of life...

The time from birth to death and the way that humans reproduce (have babies) is called a life cycle.

35

The Long and Short of it

>>all shapes and sizes>>

Breaking news! When it comes to bodies, none of us is 100% 'normal'. The simple fact is every one of us is unique—different and totally special.

From big noses to big toes, and bulgy biceps to bulgy brains, your body grows by following a set of rules laid down by your DNA. Found in every cell of your body, DNA is a code for life that's packed with between 20,000 and 30,000 instructions, called genes.

How you turn out isn't just down to DNA though; it's about environment, too. That means that the way you choose to live your life will affect your body, mind, and health.

SUPER SPIRAL

There is so much DNA in one human-body cell that, if you could stretch it out, it would measure 6½ feet.

Everyone gets two sets of DNA, one from their mother and one from their father.

You can inherit features, such as the color of your hair or eyes, from your parents. The information is carried in the DNA. That's why people usually look like other members of their family.

Unusually tall or short people may have DNA that has been damaged, or changed. Sometimes, they just inherit their height from their parents.

NOT TO BE SNIFFED AT!

Do people with big noses smell more? Better ask Mehmet Ozyurek from Turkey—his impressive honker measures an impressive 3½ inches.

Ripley's Believe It or Not!

No way!

Bao Xishun looks down on everyone he meets, because he is one of the tallest men in the world. Bao had reaching 7 feet 9 inches. Bao had a growth spurt when he was 16, which lasted for seven years. Each of Bao's legs is about 5 feet long!

He Pingping is unusually small, reaching just 2 feet 5 inches in height. He is from Mongolia and was the size of an adult's palm when he was born. His condition is caused by a change in the genes that control growth.

DOWNSIZING

When humans lose weight their fat cells don't disappear, they just get smaller.

Guddi from India is just 3 feet 2 inches tall. Despite her tiny size, Guddi gave birth to a baby measuring 19 inches.

Mind Reading

>>inside your head>>

IN THE KNOW

A person's brain at the age of 60 contains four times more information than it did at the age of 21.

Your brain is like a lump of warm jelly to touch, but don't be fooled by its cunning disguise. This unbelievable organ contains the very essence of you: your thoughts, dreams, memories, hopes, and desires. It's home to your amazing, incredible, magical mind!

This bit deals with movement.

The front of the brain is in charge of personality, thought, and behavior.

This is where the brain works on sight and hearing.

Every brain is wrapped in a bony case called a skull, which protects its 100+ billion cells. These cells can handle more than 86 million bits of information a day and your memory can hold at least 100 trillion facts during your lifetime—which is the same as a 1,000 gigabyte computer!

This area controls balance and coordination.

This bit controls sleep and growth.

This is where the brain identifies sounds.

The brain is divided into different areas with different jobs to do. For example, there are particular areas that control speech, movement, vision, and hearing.

Spinal cord

38

Stephen Wiltshire has an incredible talent for drawing and can produce remarkably accurate and detailed pictures solely from memory. In 2001, after flying in a helicopter over London, he drew in three hours an aerial illustration of a four-square-mile area of the city, featuring 12 major landmarks and 200 other buildings, all in perfect perspective and scale.

These brain cells help to feed and repair the brain. They are shaped like stars.

Brains are always busy, controlling every body part including your circulatory system, digestive system, nervous system, senses, and feelings.

Ripley's Believe It or Not!

Mentalists!

A brain weighs about 3 pounds but if all the water in it were squeezed out, it would weigh just 10 ounces!

Unborn babies grow new brain cells at the rate of 250,000 every minute!

For its size, a brain needs up to ten times more energy to work than any other organ.

The brain is one of the few body parts that cannot carry out any movements at all, since it has no muscle tissue.

There is no feeling in the human brain, only in the membrane surrounding it, which contains veins, arteries, and nerves. So a person would feel no pain from an injury to the brain alone.

Everybody can boost their brain's brilliance by reading, learning, playing, and exercising. Eating a healthy diet helps, too.

Dominic O'Brien has won the World Memory Championships eight times. In 2002, he memorized 54 packs of shuffled cards and remembered each card—all 2,808 of them—in almost perfect order. It took more than four hours to recite them, and he made just eight mistakes!

Lights Out

>>sleep>>

Your eyelids are drooping, your arms and legs feel heavy, and you know it's time to get some shut-eye. Sleep is nature's way of giving all those hard-working body parts some well-earned rest.

The good news is that when the thinking part of your brain hits the snooze button, the other parts that control important jobs—like breathing —stay wide awake!

Most people spend around one third of their lives asleep. Some of that time is spent in a deep sleep, but some of it is also spent dreaming. If you're unlucky, a few of those dreams may turn to nightmares!

LIGHT ON YOUR FEET

Shh! Don't wake your family when you need to get up in the middle of the night. Wear these slippers with flashlights in the toes and you can see where you're going without bumping into things!

You've been sitting still, doing very little, when the urge to yawn suddenly takes over. It's your body's way of getting more oxygen into your lungs, so you are ready for action.

Your brain needs sleep to be able to work properly. Without sleep you'd find it hard to think clearly, remember anything, or keep yourself safe.

NAP ATTACK

The longest anyone has survived without sleep is 18 days, 21 hours, and 40 minutes. The woeful wide awaker suffered from memory loss and hallucinations (that means seeing imaginary things).

New parents lose between 400 and 750 hours of sleep in the first year of their baby's life.

Teenagers and young children need about ten hours of sleep a night.

Snails can sleep for long periods of time—up to three years!

Stephen Hearn crashed his car at 70 mph when he was sleepwalking near Birmingham, England. When he was found, he was in his pajamas and still snoring.

Sleepwalker Lee Hadwin of North Wales is a good artist when he is asleep, but when awake he struggles to draw at all! Wandering around the house in his sleep he draws everywhere, even on walls and tables!

1st it!

Your eyelids close when you are feeling drowsy. When you dream your eyeballs flick from side to side.

SNORE!
The back of your mouth and throat relax and may partly block your airways, leading to that pig-snuffle snoring sound!

GROW!
While you snooze your body can repair itself and put spare energy into growing.

DREAM!
No one really knows why we dream, but it may help us to organize our thoughts and remember things.

RELAX!
Your muscles relax. When you dream, the ability to move your limbs is (usually) switched off, which stops you from acting out your dreams. If this doesn't happen you may find yourself sleepwalking.

WAY TO GLOW!
A pillow with a built-in light allows its users to read in bed and also acts as an alarm clock. The light can be set to come on gradually at the time you want to wake up. The increasing lightness acts like a sunrise and wakes up sleepyheads in a more natural way than the blare of an alarm or radio.

ICE HOTEL!!
Fancy sleeping on an ice bed? You can do this in Shimukappu, Japan, where an ice hotel caters for sleeping, eating, and bathing—all on ice.

ANIMALS SLEEP TOO
Pythons sleep for around 18 hours out of 24, but sheep only need about four hours of sleep.

Under Attack

You may not know it, but your body is engaged in a deadly battle with the world, right now! It's true—there are plenty of bugs, bacteria, and other baddies out there, just waiting to do you harm.

Your body fights attackers 24/7. From your tough outer layer (skin) to spit, strong stomach juices, bacteria in your gut, hair in your nose, and tears in your eyes, there are lots of clever defense systems in place.

Thankfully, the human body has evolved over millions of years to repel most invaders. Your body has an amazing ability to defend itself, and even repair damage done to it. Without this ability even a simple cold could spell the end of you. Of course, we can't always do it alone, so it's time to say a big "thank you" to doctors!

BIG WORD ALERT!

IMMUNE SYSTEM

Your body has an immune system, which makes white blood cells that attack and kill invaders, such as the virus that causes flu.

A VIRUS ATTACKS THE BLOOD STREAM
BUG ALERT!

Vomiting, sneezing, crying, spitting, coughing, and diarrhea (runny feces) are all ways of ejecting stuff your body doesn't like.

TASTY!

These tiny fish nibble at dead skin on customers' feet at a spa resort in Japan, and leave the feet clean and refreshed!

TOASTY!

Stand back! This fire treatment is popular in China to help prevent colds and flu.

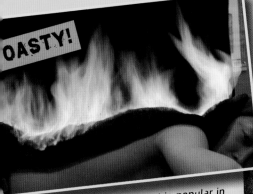

MUDDY!

It's a dirty business in these mud baths, which are meant to ease pain and diseases.

KILL OR CURE

In ancient times, headaches and other medical problems were sometimes cured by drilling holes into the skull. Known as "trepanation" this operation is still carried out in some parts of the world today.

Maggots are sometimes used to treat infected skin and tissues, which they eat. Because they don't eat healthy flesh, these greedy grubs help wounds to heal before life-threatening infections, such as gangrene, can set in.

A pair of spiders set up home inside the ear canal of nine-year-old Jesse Courtney from America. Thankfully, doctors were able to extract the eight-legged invaders, and no harm was done.

Over 2,000 years ago, Hippocrates, a doctor, told his patients to chew on bark from a willow tree when they were in pain. We now use an ingredient found in willow bark to make aspirin!

Muntoyib, an Indonesian bee-sting therapist, covers himself with hundreds of live honeybees in India. Some people think that bee venom injected from live stinging bees helps to treat chronic pain.

twist it!

in the olden days

Before modern medical science took over, people invented some weird ways to get better.

CATCH THAT SHREW!

Aching bones were treated with the help of a dead shrew. Sufferers were told to keep the furry little creatures in their pockets.

DON'T BE AN ASS!

Passing a child under the belly of a donkey three times was said to cure whooping cough.

HOT AND STEAMING!

If you had TB (a deadly chest disease) you'd be told to kill a cow, stick your head into its warm body, and breathe in deeply.

TOM FOR YOUR TUM!

One of the first types of tomato ketchup was used to cure diarrhea in the 1800s.

OLD BONES

In some Chinese villages, dinosaur bones are ground up to make a paste. It's used to treat dizziness and leg cramps!

43

Fit for Life

>>take care>>

There's no such thing as a perfect human, but keeping your body bits in tip-top shape has got to make good sense.

The human body is like a machine with lots of working parts. It needs to be taken care of, and that means exercise and a good diet. There are around six billion humans on the planet, and many of them, from super-sized sumo wrestlers to bendy-bodied yogis, keep the power switch turned to maximum.

For kids, it's easy to keep it fun. All you've got to do is play, eat well, and sleep. But for some groaning grown-ups, it's a hard, sweaty slog keeping those muscles and bones in peak condition.

GULP!

Water makes up 60% of y• body weight. It's the liquic of life, so drink up. Your bon• and teeth are packed wi• calcium—there's loads • this mighty mineral in mi•

GRUB!

Veggies and fruit are grea• grub. At least one-third o• a human's diet should be• made up of these super foods.

GO FOR IT!

Squash (the hard-hitting racquet and ball game) has been voted the healthiest sport ever, beating running, swimming, and basketball into first place.

FITNESS FUN

Hula hooping is a hu-lotta fun! Alesya Goulevich spun 100 hula hoops at the same time, at the Big Apple Circus in Boston in 2004.

SURF'S UP!

Surfers are super-fit because they use almost every muscle in their bodies to stay balanced and upright on their boards.

PUSHING IT

Ashrita Furman, a health-food store manager from New York City, is super fit. Amongst his amazing feats are climbing Mount Fuji on a pogo stick, hula hooping with a 14½ feet hoop, and doing 9,628 sit ups in an hour. Here, he's pushing an orange along for one mile using his nose!

Kids should be exercising for at least 60 minutes every day. Running, walking, cycling, and playing sports all keep you fit for life.

stick with it!

Kyle Nolte from Arkansas has got so good at jumping on his pogo stick, he can also play baseball, hula hoop, or skip whilst pogoing!

FITNESS FANATICS

Tirtha Kumar Phani from India ran more than 37 miles every day, for one year. He clocked up a blistering 14,031 miles in total!

Cycling backward is a popular sport in some parts of the world. Riders sit on the handlebars and pedal in reverse.

Aged 91, Ervin Ashley of the USA climbed 2,000 steps every day to keep in shape!

You're never too young to get fit! In 2006, 1,100 babies took part in a crawling marathon. The mini racers had to crawl along a 16-foot track, and the young winner was rewarded with a bag of baby goodies!

twist it!

INDEX

46

ACKNOWLEDGMENTS

COVER (l) © Sebastian Kaulitzki – istockphoto.com, (r) Lilli Strauss/AP/PA Photos; **2** Raymond w. Gonzales; **3** (l) © Peter Galbraith – Fotolia.com; **4** © Sebastian Kaulitzki – istockphoto.com; **5** (r) Maria Laura Antonelli/Rex Features, (b) Lilli Strauss/AP/PA Photos; **6–7** (dp) © AlienCat – Fotolia.com; **7** (b/l) Raymond W Gonzales, (b/r) Simon De Trey-White/ Barcroft Media; **8** (l) © Peter Galbraith – Fotolia.com, (r) © AlienCat – Fotolia.com; **9** (l, b) ChinaFotoPress/Photocome/ PA Photos; **10** (sp) © V. Yakobchuk – Fotolia.com; **11** (c) © Sebastian Kaulitzki – istockphoto.com, (r) © Wong Sze Fei – Fotolia.com; **13** (l) © Roman Dekan – Fotolia.com, (t/r) AP Photo/Rubin Museum of Art, Diane Bondareff, (b/r) Jeff Chen/Trigger images; **14** © saginbay – Fotolia.com; **15** (t) © Xtremer – Fotolia.com, (b/r) © saginbay – Fotolia.com; **17** (l) Patrick Hertzog/AFP/Getty Images, (c) Prakash Hatvalne/AP/PA Photos, (r) Reuters/Christina Hu; **18–19** (b/c) © ktsdesign – Fotolia.com; **18** (t/r) Paul Cooper/Rex Features; **19** (t/l) Reuters/Seth Wenig, (b/r) Camera Press/Terje Eggum/Scanpix; **21** (l) Manichi Rafi, (c) Steven Heward/ toothartist.com, (r) Fabian Bimmer/AP/PA Photos; **22** (l) Dr. Kessel & Dr. Kardon/Tissues & Organs/Getty Images, (r) Reuters/Staff Photographer; **23** (t/l) Stan Honda/AFP/Getty Images, (b/l) Matt Cardy/Getty Images, (r) Nils Jorgensen/Rex Features; **24–25** (c) © Mark Kostich – istockphoto.com; **25** (b/l) Sipa Press/Rex Features, (b/c) Phil Noble/PA Archive/PA Photos, (b/r) Reuters/STR New; **27** (l) Dan Burton/underwaterimages.co.uk, (t/r) John Bavosi/Science Photo Library, (b/r) Gabriel Bouys/AFP/Getty Images; **28** (l) © Sebastian Kaulitzki – Fotolia.com; **29** (l) Roger Bamber/Rex Features, (r) Tim Barnsley/Armidale Express; **30** (r) NBCUPhotobank/Rex Features; **31** (l) Ian Waldie/Rex Features, (r) Scott Barbour/Getty Images; **32** (l) Jean/Empics Entertainment, (r) Thanh Nien Newspaper/ AP/PA Photos; **33** (l) Rex Features, (r) Tao-Chuan Yeh/AFP/Getty Images; **34** (r) Reuters/Ho New; **35** (l) Reuters/Victor Ruiz, (r) George A. Blair; **36–37** (dp) Reuters/ China Daily China Daily Information Corp; **36** (l) © Dmitry Sunagatov – Fotolia.com, (t/r) IHA/UPPA/Photoshot; **37** (t) © Sasha Radosavljevic – istockphoto.com; **39** (t) Gary Bishop/Rex Features, (b) Greg Williams/Rex Features, (r) © Sebastian Kaulitzki – Fotolia.com; **40–41** (dp) © Veronika Vasilyuk – Fotolia.com, (b/c) Reuters/Kim Kyung Hoon; **40** (c) Rex Features; **41** (c) Solent News/Rex Features; **42** (sp) © David Marchal – istockphoto.com; **43** (t/l) Reuters/Larry Downing,(c/l) Chu Yongzhi/ChinaFotoPress/GettyImages, (b/l) Reuters/China Daily China Daily Information Corp – CDIC, (b/r) Reuters/Beawiharta Beawiharta; **44–45** (b) Reuters/Sergio Moraes; **44** (t) Boston Herald/Rex Features; **45** (l) Reuters/Shannon Stapleton.

Key: t = top, b = bottom, c = center, l = left, r = right, sp = single page, dp = double page, bgd = background

All other photos are from Ripley Entertainment Inc.

All artwork by Janet Baker & Julian Baker (JB Illustrations)

Every attempt has been made to acknowledge correctly and contact copyright holders and we apologize in advance for any unintentional errors or omissions, which will be corrected in future editions.